TOTALLY STUPID MEN

Hysterical home truths about the men in your life

Michael O'Mara Books Limited

First published in Great Britain in 1997 by
Michael O'Mara Books Limited
9 Lion Yard
Tremadoc Road
London SW4 7NQ

A CIP catalogue record for this book is available from the British Library

ISBN 1-85479-274-1

1 3 5 7 9 10 8 6 4 2

Designed by Mick Keates
Typeset by Concise Artisans

Printed in England by Cox & Wyman, Reading

What do you call a fisherman?

A jerk on one line waiting for a jerk on the other.

Why don't women work as long and hard as men in the office?

They do it right the first time.

Why are male brains considered a better donation to science?

They haven't been used.

How can you recognise a stupid man's pencil?

It has a rubber at both ends.

A man's first experience of life is trying to get out of a woman's body and then he spends the rest of his life trying to get back in.

I hate men who...

talk out of the back of their heads

Why are men like bank accounts?

One day they're up,
the next they're down,
and most of the time
they show no interest.

My husband is so sensitive
about his hair.
I don't know why...
he hasn't got any.

Man:

What would you say if I asked you to marry me?

Woman:

Nothing, I can't laugh and talk at the same time.

Did you hear about the guy who was so stupid he had to drop his trousers to count to 21?

Why do men complain women have no sense of humour when they have no sense and even less humour?

More husbands would leave home if they knew how to pack.

How does a stupid man make sex more interesting?

He leaves town.

One girlfriend said to another girlfriend, 'My most secret fantasy is having two men at once.'

'Really, why?' asked the other.

'One for cooking, the other for cleaning.'

My husband is a self-made man
and he worships his creator.

Two stupid workmen were digging out a quarry with a gigantic excavator. One said to the other, 'It's a crying shame; this quarry would provide work for a thousand men with shovels.'

The other replied, 'Or a million men with teaspoons.'

I hate men who…

say, 'trust me!'

What three little words will you never hear a stupid man say?

It's on me.

How can you recognise a stupid man's helicopter?

It has an ejection seat.

Why did the stupid man go parachuting?

Who knows why he does anything?

How does a stupid man cook dinner?

I don't know, he's never done it.

Why do stupid men think they're so clever?

Who cares?

How do you spot a stupid pirate?

He has a patch over both eyes.

Down at the pub one stupid man was talking to another: 'What has six balls and screws you twice a week?'

'I dunno know, what?' slurped the other.

'The Lottery.'

When the stupid man says he takes life with a pinch of salt, it's true . . . it's just that he takes it with a slice of lemon and a shot of tequila, too.

A man marries a woman hoping she'll never change and a woman marries a man hoping he will.

What is the first prize in the stupid man's lottery?

£10 a year for a million years.

What do people say when a stupid man enters a room with a beautiful woman on his arm?

'Where did you get the tattoo?'

Men don't get excited about women's minds, they get excited about what they don't mind.

What does it mean to come home to a man who'll give you some love and tenderness?

You're in the wrong house.

How do dumb men define a sharing relationship?

They eat – we cook.

Wife:

Who was that woman I saw kissing you last night?

Husband:

What time was it?

I hate men who…

pick their teeth

Why is a stupid man like a microwave?

Thirty seconds and he's finished.

Why do men act like idiots?

Who says they're acting?

How do you find out what life is like without a man around?

Get married.

What's the difference between an intelligent man and a stupid man?

Nothing, they both think they know everything.

Why doesn't a stupid man believe in the new Messiah?

Because to him a second coming is an impossibility.

Did you hear about the man who makes love like he drives his car?

He goes too fast and gets there before anyone else.

How can you tell if a man is lying?

His lips are moving.

Why are all the dumb blonde jokes one-liners?

So men can understand them.

Husband:

Let's go out and have some fun tonight.

Wife:

Okay, but if you get home before I do, just remember to leave the front door open.

A man came home and found his wife in bed with his best friend. 'What are you doing?' he shouted.

'See?' she said to her lover. 'Didn't I tell you he was stupid?'

You don't need to lead a man into temptation – he can usually find it on his own.

What do you call a man who tidies up after himself?

An over-achiever.

Not all women are silly – some are single.

Why is a man like a food processor?

You know you need one but you're not quite sure why.

What's the best way to keep a stupid man happy in the bedroom?

Put the TV in the bedroom and turn on the football.

How do you keep a stupid man from wanting sex?

Marry him.

I hate men who...

leave the seat up (among other things)

Why did the stupid man throw away his toilet brush?

He discovered toilet paper.

What are the ups and down of marriage?

The toilet seat is always up and his interest is always down.

Plumber:

Where's the drip?

Wife:

He's in the bathroom trying to fix the leak.

How do you keep a stupid man from wanting the other woman?

Divorce him.

How do you lose fourteen stone of fat?

Divorce him.

What does a stupid man do when confronted by a toddler having a tantrum?

Stamps his feet and shouts for mother.

What do you call a stupid man who uses the rhythm method?

Dad.

What's the definition of a well-informed man?

Someone who agrees with you.

How many men does it take to milk a cow?

Twenty-four; one on each teat and twenty to lift the cow up and down.

A woman, at any age, likes a man with a will of his own – made out in her favour of course.

How does a stupid man count money?

1,2,3,4,5, another, another, another…

How do we know Adam was stupid?

Would a clever man eat an apple when a naked woman was discussing temptation?

Love, companionship and sex are the three things a woman needs from a man. By the time a woman comes of age she knows she will have to go to three different places for it.

The science teacher came in and addressed one of her students: 'Can you tell me which portion of the human anatomy swells ten times its normal size during periods of agitation or emotional excitement?'

Blushing, the shy girl stammered, 'I-I would rather n-not answer that q-question.'

Arching a brow the teacher asked, 'Oh? And why not?'

'Well, it's too embarrassing to say.' said the student.

'Not at all!' huffed the teacher, 'The correct answer is the pupil of the eyes, and your response tells me two things: first, that you didn't read last night's homework and second that marriage is going to leave you a tremendously disappointed young woman.'

I hate men who...

swirl drinks with their fingers

Women at forty are at their best, but men of forty are too stupid to realise it.

What's the best way to get a man to remember your anniversary?

Get married on his birthday.

Is an IQ of 180 considered high?

No, not when you consider it's the total IQ of eight men.

How is a stupid man like a python?

No sane person would go to bed with either of them.

After struggling to open his beer the man leaned over to the cocktail waitress: 'Excuse me, I was wondering if you could help me out?'

'Certainly,' smiled the waitress, 'go right through that door.'

'Yes,' said the man to his barber, 'split hair is a problem. Mine split about five years ago.'

How did the stupid man die drinking milk?

The cow fell on him.

Husband to wife:
'Honey, do you think these trousers need altering, are they too big on me?'

'No, they don't need altering, but you do.'

How many stupid men does it take to change the toilet paper roll?

Don't know, it's never happened before.

How do you know a fax is from a stupid man?

There's a stamp on it.

Wife to her husband:
'Honey, why don't you take up jogging again? It's the only time I ever get to hear your heavy breathing.'

'Perhaps,' suggested the shop assistant, 'your wife might like some cucumber soap for her birthday?'

'I don't think so,' he replied, 'she just rinses them off with water.'

The husband walked over to the perfume counter and told the shop assistant he'd like a bottle of Chanel No.5 for his wife's birthday.

'A little surprise?' smiled the clerk.

'You bet,' answered the husband, 'she's expecting an all-expenses-paid trip to New York.'

What's a stupid man's idea of a varied diet?

A quarter-pounder with cheese one day and without cheese the next.

Why don't stupid men's dogs do tricks?

You have to be more intelligent than a dog to teach it tricks.

My husband takes the biscuit. Whenever we go to a new hotel room, he insists on taking home the soap and shampoo from the bathroom. One night I caught him walking down the hall trick-or-treating.

No, my husband takes the biscuit. We bought these new car phones that give you thirty minutes of free call time on the weekends. I went down to the garage to look for my husband. He was sitting in the car talking to his best friend with an egg timer on the dashboard.

A man walks into the chemist, 'Can I buy some male protection?' he enquires. 'How much does it cost?'

'That'll be £5.00 including tax.' said the shopkeeper.

'Ah,' said the man, 'I always wondered how you keep them up.'

I hate men who...

ogle

The bookshop assistant was talking to his new trainee: 'Did you see that new book *50 Ways to Mate*, translated from Russian with 100 illustrations, it's practically running out of the shop... I've never seen a book on chess sell so well.'

Wife to her husband:
'Honey, why are you home so early?'

'Well, I'm so mad – I had a fight with my boss and he wouldn't take back what he said.'

'What did he say?' said the shocked wife.

'You're fired!'

Why did the stupid man buy an electric lawnmower?

So he could find his way back to the house.

How are men like dogs about housework?

They run and hide every time they see a vacuum cleaner.

I hate men who…

spread out on public transport

A woman went into the pet shop to confront the owner, Barney: 'I want to return this cat. You said it was good for mice, but all it does is lie there.'

'So,' he replied, 'isn't that good for mice?'

Why do stupid men write T.G.I.F. on their shoes?

To tell them: 'Toes go in first.'

How can you tell if a stupid man is cheating on you?

He has a bath more than once a month.

'Do you think you could fall for me?' asked the man at the bar.

'Only if you pushed me.'

Why do stupid men drive BMWs?

Because they can spell it.

What's the difference between a man and a shopping trolley?

A shopping trolley has a mind of its own.

Why did the stupid man get a stabbing pain in his eye every time he drank a cup of tea?

He forgot to take the spoon out.

What do you call a stupid man with headphones on?

Anything you like, he can't hear you.

What do you see when you look into a stupid man's eyes?

The back of his head.

I hate men who…

wear mirrored sunglasses

A woman and her stupid husband were having a tea party. 'Put out the sugar tongs,' she told him. 'Otherwise your filthy friends will go to the loo, pee all over their fingers and then handle the sugar cubes.' After the party the wife complained that the sugar tongs weren't on the table.

'On the table?' her husband cried. 'I put them in the toilet!'

I hate men who…

never use deodorant

An Englishman, a Scotsman and an Irishman were all sentenced to death by firing squad. The Englishman was brought out first and the firing squad took aim, when suddenly the Englishman yelled out, 'AVALANCHE!' In the confusion that followed he escaped. Next the Scotsman thought he would try something similar. As the firing squad took aim he yelled, 'FLOOD!', and he too made his escape. Finally, it was the Irishman's turn. Confident of following in his friends' footsteps, as the firing squad took aim, he yelled, 'FIRE!'

How do you confuse a stupid man?

You don't, they're born that way.

When I asked my fiancé this morning why his coffee tasted like mud, he said that's perfectly natural, honey, after all it was only ground this morning.

What's black and fuzzy and hangs from the ceiling?

A stupid electrician.

In a room full of interesting people what is the only thing a stupid man sees?

The bimbo and his rival.

'I'd like to be included in your next edition.' said the guy on the phone to the Guinness Book of Records.

'Why, what have you done?' came the reply.

'I've completed a paint-by-number in just under a week and on the box it said three to five years.'

A wife yelled at her husband when he came home late from work again, 'You should've been here at 6 o'clock!'

He replied, 'Why, what happened?'

How do you know when your boyfriend is really stupid?

When he knows what he wants but he can't spell it.

'Doctor, doctor, I have a real problem down under. I keep thinking I'm getting smaller.'

'Why? I can't see anything down there.'

How many men does it take to change a lightbulb?

Ten – one to put it in and nine to congratulate him down the pub.

When do men insist that women are illogical?

When a woman doesn't agree with them.

Why does a stupid man have a hole in his pocket?

So he can count to six.

My husband says he has a wonderful personality... he's obviously saving it for a special occasion.

Did you hear about the family who sent their son to summer camp?

The boy wrote home he had grown another foot so his father knitted him another sock.

You can't change a man... even if you could, the only person who would appreciate it is his next wife.

Two men were passengers on a four-engine plane. Suddenly one engine failed and the pilot announced that the plane would now be fifteen minutes late. A short time later another engine failed. The pilot announced they would be thirty minutes late. Then the third engine failed and the pilot announced that they would be one hour late.

At this point one man said to the other, 'If the fourth engine quits we could be up here all day.'

While driving through the back roads, two stupid lorry drivers came to a bridge with a sign on it that read, 'CLEARANCE 11' 3"'.

They got out and measured the lorry and it was 12' 4" tall.

'What do you think?' said one to the other.

The driver looked around and replied, 'Not a policeman in sight. Let's take a chance.'

What's the difference between a baby and your husband?

You can leave a baby alone with the babysitter.

What quality do most men look for in a woman?

Breathing.

I hate men who…

wear sandals and socks

Where's the safest place to hide money from your husband?

Under the soap.

How do you brainwash a man?

Step on his enema bag.

Did you hear about the stupid man who thought he was a half-breed?

His father was a man and his mother was a woman.

What is special about a stupid man's parachute?

It opens on impact.

A woman came into the police station to report her husband missing and described him as '29 years old, 6 feet 3 inches tall, blonde and handsome.'

'I knew your husband.' said the desk sergeant. 'He was bald, fat and forty.'

'I know,' the woman replied, 'but who wants HIM back?'

A man was visiting his barber and as a special treat the barber pulled out his new home brew of hair tonic to use on his customer.

'Hey, don't do that,' shouted the customer, 'my wife will think I smell like a brothel.'

Another customer who was eavesdropping jumped in, 'I don't mind, when it's my turn you can load me up on the stuff – my wife doesn't know what a brothel smells like.'

In the sports shop a golfer was talking to the shop owner. 'You know, it isn't such a good deal to get my golf balls here anymore. I can go to New York and get a whole box for five dollars.'

'Yeah,' said the owner, 'but what about the airfare?'

Did you hear about the man who didn't know which way the lift was going even though they gave him two guesses?

Did you hear about the farmer who ran a steamroller across his fields because he wanted to market mashed potatoes?

A guy shows up at his date's apartment soaking wet. When she opens the door she can't believe her eyes: 'Why is your shirt dripping with water?' she exclaims.

'Well, the label said "Wash-n-Wear",' he replies.

I hate men who…

wipe cutlery on the tablecloth

Why did the stupid man lose his job as a lift attendant?

He couldn't learn the route.

After being married for years, one night a couple were making love and the husband asked 'I didn't hurt you, darling, did I?'

'No,' she replied, 'why do you ask?'

'You moved.'

A handyman was invited into a wealthy businessman's home to build some shelves in his library. 'That's a nice moosehead you've got on the wall. Any chance I can go into the next room and see the rest of it?'

Why couldn't the stupid man make ice cubes?

He lost the recipe.

Did you hear about the stupid newly-wed who didn't know the difference between Vaseline and putty?

His windows fell out.

Why did the stupid newly-wed stay up all night?

He was waiting for his sexual relations.

What's the only time a man thinks about a candlelight dinner?

When the power goes off.

What did God say after he created Eve?

Practice makes perfect.

How are men like carpet tiles?

If you lay them properly the first time around, you can walk all over them for the rest of your life.

Why does a man only get half-hour lunch-breaks?

So his boss doesn't have to retrain him.

What one thing did God do right when he created man?

He created woman to explain the difference between his black and navy blue socks.

There was a man so stupid he didn't know arson from incest.

He set his sister on fire.

I hate men who…

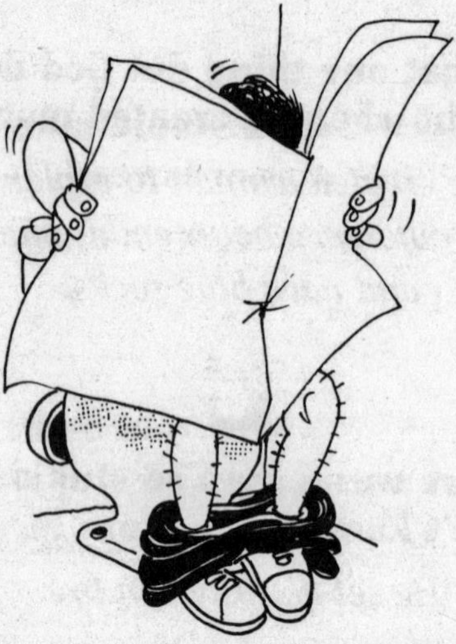

disappear into the loo for hours at a time

How does a stupid man know dinner is ready?

The smoke alarm goes off.

How did the wife stop her stupid husband biting his nails?

She made him wear shoes.

What is the best birth-control device for a stupid man?

His face.

Did you hear about the man who was raking up leaves in his garden?

He fell out of the tree.

What's the useless piece of skin attached to the male member?

A man.

Why do so few men end up in Heaven?

They never stop to ask directions.

What's the only exercise men are good at?

Sucking in their stomachs every time they see a bikini.

I wouldn't say he's handsome. I wouldn't, but he would.

How do stupid people reproduce?

They exchange underwear.

What does a stupid man say when he proposes marriage?

'You are going to have a WHAT?'

One girlfriend to another:
It seems that common sense would prevent a lot divorces.
The other:
Yes, and a lot of marriages, too.

'Mummy,' said the stupid boy,
'I have the biggest willie
in the third form. Is it because
I'm advanced?'

'No,' said mother,
'it's because you're fifteen.'

Why did the stupid man put his willie in boiling water?

His wife told him to get sterilised.

How do you make a stupid man's eyes twinkle?

Shine a torch in his ear.

'Daddy, can you make a noise like a frog?' asked the stupid man's son.

'Why do you ask that?' said his father.

'Because Mummy said that she'll be glad when you croak.'

The great thing about being a stupid man is you can hide your own Easter egg.

What do we women have to do . . . paint a bull's eye in the toilet bowl in order to get him to aim it in there?

'Mummy, what happens when a car gets too old and rusty to work?' the little girl asked.

'Well,' her mother said, 'someone sells it to your father.'

What do you call a man who supports a woman's career, helps prepare dinner, bathes the kids, and earns a six-figure income?

Darling.

'Am I your first?' asked the Latin lover after sex.

'You might be,' she replied, 'you look familiar.'

What do toilets and anniversaries have in common?

Men always miss them.

'Does your husband play cards for money?'

'No, but the men he plays against do.'

'Did you hear about the stupid farmer who traded his only horse for a bale of hay?'

'What does he intend to do with the hay?'

'He's going to see if he can borrow back the horse long enough to get rid of it.'

'How did you meet your boyfriend?'

'I was crossing a street when this car drove up and stopped with a big jerk. It was him.'

How do we know that Adam was a stupid man?

Because he came first – they all do.

What does a man really mean when he says he's separated from his wife?

She's at home with the children, and I'm here, alone, with you.

How can you tell if a stupid man cooked dinner?

The salad's burnt.

How are men like dogs?

One stroke, and they follow you everywhere.

Why is swapping partners with your friend a bad mistake?

Because it's so depressing when you get him back.

What do you call a man who opens the car door for you?

A chauffeur.

What happened when the stupid man telephoned the sex-chat line?

The girl said 'Not tonight. I've got earache.'

What do you call ten stupid men in a circle?

A dope ring.

Man:

Do you want to come up for a nightcap?

Woman:

Why, hasn't anyone ever had sex with you sober?

Why do some men like tying a woman to the bed?

Because otherwise they'd run once they'd seen him.

I hate men who...

break wind in bed

The stupid man was filling out a form. When he came to the question 'sex', there were two boxes marked 'M' and 'F'. After thinking for a moment he ticked both boxes and wrote, 'also on Wednesdays occasionally'.

At the end of the first act, the wife stopped her husband from leaving the theatre. 'Didn't you like the first act?' she asked.

'Oh, I liked it alright,' he said, 'but the programme says the second act takes place two weeks later.'

What's the difference between woman's bra size and a man's IQ?

Nothing, they're both the same.

Did you hear about the man who died at the height of passion?

He came and went at the same time.

The stupid man joined the police. On his first day he was given an intelligence test. The last question was: Who killed Jesus Christ?

'Great,' he thought, 'my first day and they expect me to solve a murder!'

Did you hear about the stupid Olympic skier who was so proud of his gold medal he had it bronzed?

Did you hear about the stupid kidnapper?

He enclosed a stamped, self-addressed envelope with the ransom note.

A man visits his doctor:
'Doctor, doctor, I haven't been feeling myself today.'

'It's a good thing,' came the reply, 'that's an awful habit.'

'Did you know that all night long you were cursing me in my sleep?' said the husband to his wife.

'Who said I was sleeping?'

I hate men who...

practise imaginary golf swings

When the stupid man's grandfather died, he rang the local newspaper to print the death notice. 'That will be £25 per inch.' the clerk said.

'I can't afford that,' said the dope, 'he was six foot four.'

'Mrs Hardy, the court is going to see to it that you receive £1,500 a month in alimony.'

'Thanks judge,' said Mr Hardy, 'I'll be sure to give her a few bob myself.'

A wise person once said that a woman is incomplete until she's married . . . and then she's finished.

'I'm delighted with the doctor's physical, dear. He said I have the breasts of a woman half my age.'

'Yeah, but what did he say about your sixty-year-old ass?'

'Come to think of it, he didn't even mention your name.'

Wife to her husband:
'Did you know that drinking makes you handsome dear?'

'But I don't drink.' he said, puzzled.

'No,' she smiled, 'but I do.'

Did you hear about the guy who rushed his pregnant wife to the pizza parlour because he heard they advertised free deliveries?

'Mummy, what's a pauper?'

'Why that's another name for father, dear.'

Did you hear about the dumb guy who went to the luggage shop and asked for seven overnight cases?

He was going away for a week.

The stupid man's wife complained that he was no use in bed so he consulted his doctor.

'You're in terrible shape.' said the doc. 'Give up the booze and fags and run ten miles a day. Your wife will be amazed.'

Two weeks later he phoned the doctor to tell him it worked, he was in great shape.

'Is your wife amazed?' asked the doc.

'How would I know? I'm 150 miles from home.'